Very BRITISH WIT

QUIPS AND QUOTES TO SUIT
ALL MANNER OF OCCASIONS

Richard Benson

summersdale

VERY BRITISH WIT

First published as *Wit of the Nation*

This revised edition copyright © Summersdale Publishers Ltd, 2015

Illustrations © Shutterstock

Summersdale Publishers Ltd
46 West Street
Chichester
West Sussex
PO19 1RP
UK

www.summersdale.com

Printed and bound in the Czech Republic

ISBN: 978-1-84953-777-3

Substantial discounts on bulk quantities of Summersdale books are available to corporations, professional associations and other organisations. For details contact Nicky Douglas by telephone: +44 (0) 1243 756902, fax: +44 (0) 1243 786300 or email: nicky@summersdale.com.

Contents

Editor's Note..5

Best of British..6

Fur, Feather and Fin.......................................17

Culture Vultures...26

Eye of the Beholder..36

Under the Covers..47

Prattle of the Sexes...56

Below the Belt..67

Cutting a Dash...78

To Have and To Hold......................................86

With Friends Like That....................................94

It's What You Make It.....................................103

Thicker Than Water.......................................111

By the Book...117

Johnny Foreigner..127

When Their Lips Move....................................135

Head Over Heels...146

Mind Your Ps and Qs.....................................154

The Curse of the Drinking Classes....................160

Well, If You Ask Me…....................................167

Vice and Virtue..175

Drunk as a Lord...185

The Youth of Today..193

The Way of All Flesh......................................200

Editor's Note

When it comes to belly-aching witticisms, no one does it quite like the Brits.

This wonderful nation has been witness to centuries of dry politicians, cut-throat comedians, hilarious writers and a whole host of other fabulously funny people just waiting to be quoted by the rest of us.

There comes a time when we're all looking for that classic one-liner to brighten up a dull wedding speech, impart knowledge to our children or simply make us sound far funnier than we actually are. If that time is now, you're holding the right book.

To save you trawling through a lifetime of literature, we've compiled the cream of the cackle-worthy crop for you to feast on. Nestled in the pages of this quotable collection are wry remarks, poignant ponderings and ticklesome treats to suit all manner of occasions.

Neatly organised into subject sections ranging from art and advice to families, friends and foreigners, the hardest thing left for you to do is pick your favourites.

So sit back, relax and prepare to free your stiff upper lip – a good old British smirk is just a page away.

Best

OF

BRITISH

MY CHILDREN ARE NOT
ROYAL; THEY JUST HAPPEN
TO HAVE THE QUEEN
FOR THEIR AUNT.

Princess Margaret

....

It took me 20 years of studied self-
restraint, aided by the natural decay
of my faculties, to make myself dull
enough to be accepted as a serious
person by the British public.

George Bernard Shaw

....

MY VOCAL CORDS ARE MADE
OF TWEED. I GIVE OFF AN AIR
OF OXFORD DONNISHNESS
AND OLD BBC WIRELESSES.

Stephen Fry

An Irishman fights before he reasons, a Scotchman reasons before he fights, an Englishman is not particular as to the order of precedence, but will do either to accommodate his customers.

Charles Caleb Colton

....

AMERICAN-STYLE ICED TEA IS THE PERFECT DRINK FOR A HOT, SUNNY DAY. IT'S NEVER REALLY CAUGHT ON IN THE UK, PROBABLY BECAUSE THE LAST TIME WE HAD A HOT, SUNNY DAY WAS BACK IN 1957.

Tom Holt

The land of

EMBARRASSMENT

AND BREAKFAST.

Julian Barnes on Britain

Life is unliveable to them unless they have tea and puddings.

George Orwell on the English

....

THE MONARCHY IS SO EXTRAORDINARILY USEFUL. WHEN BRITAIN WINS A BATTLE SHE SHOUTS, 'GOD SAVE THE QUEEN'; WHEN SHE LOSES SHE VOTES DOWN THE PRIME MINISTER.

Winston Churchill

....

The whole strength of England lies in the fact that the enormous majority of the English people are snobs.

George Bernard Shaw

THE ENGLISH CONTRIBUTION TO WORLD CUISINE – THE CHIP.

John Cleese

....

Oats. A grain, which in England is generally given to horses, but in Scotland supports the people.

Samuel Johnson

....

THE IRISH ARE HEARTY, THE SCOTCH PLAUSIBLE, THE FRENCH POLITE, THE GERMANS GOOD-NATURED, THE ITALIANS COURTLY, THE SPANIARDS RESERVED AND DECOROUS – THE ENGLISH ALONE SEEM TO EXIST IN TAKING AND GIVING OFFENCE.

William Hazlitt

I've sometimes thought... that the difference between us and the English is that the Scotch are hard in all other respects but soft with women, and the English are hard with women but soft in all other respects.

J. M. Barrie

....

I THINK THE BRITISH HAVE THE DISTINCTION ABOVE ALL OTHER NATIONS OF BEING ABLE TO PUT NEW WINE INTO OLD BOTTLES WITHOUT BURSTING THEM.

Clement Attlee

What two ideas are
more inseparable than
beer and Britannia?

Sydney Smith

There's nothing the British like better than a bloke who comes from nowhere, makes it, and then gets clobbered.

Melvyn Bragg

....

IT IS ILLEGAL IN ENGLAND TO STATE IN PRINT THAT A WIFE CAN AND SHOULD DERIVE SEXUAL PLEASURE FROM INTERCOURSE.

Bertrand Russell

....

The Welsh are not meant to go out in the sun. They start to photosynthesise.

Rhys Ifans

SCOTLAND HAS THE ONLY FOOTBALL TEAM IN THE WORLD THAT DOES A LAP OF DISGRACE.

Billy Connolly

....

Only in Britain could it be thought a defect to be 'too clever by half'. The probability is that too many people are too stupid by three-quarters.

John Major

....

WHAT ENGLISHMAN WILL GIVE HIS MIND TO POLITICS AS LONG AS HE CAN AFFORD TO KEEP A MOTOR CAR?

George Bernard Shaw

The maxim of the

BRITISH PEOPLE IS

'BUSINESS AS USUAL'.

Winston Churchill

Fur,
FEATHER
AND FIN

Animals are such agreeable friends – they ask no questions, they pass no criticisms.

George Eliot

....

A HORSE IS DANGEROUS
AT BOTH ENDS AND
UNCOMFORTABLE
IN THE MIDDLE.

Ian Fleming

....

A dog is not intelligent.
Never trust an animal that's surprised by its own farts.

Frank Skinner

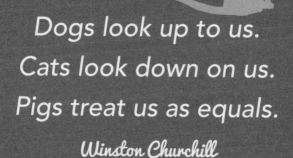

Dogs look up to us.
Cats look down on us.
Pigs treat us as equals.

Winston Churchill

IN ANCIENT TIMES CATS WERE
WORSHIPPED AS GODS; THEY
HAVE NOT FORGOTTEN THIS.

Terry Pratchett

....

I didn't just grow
up with horses;
I wanted to be one.

Clare Balding

....

YOU THINK DOGS WILL
NOT BE IN HEAVEN? I TELL
YOU, THEY WILL BE THERE
LONG BEFORE ANY OF US.

Robert Louis Stevenson

When my cats aren't happy, I'm not happy. Not because I care about their mood but because I know they're just sitting there thinking up ways to get even.

Percy Bysshe Shelley

....

MAN IS AN ANIMAL THAT MAKES BARGAINS: NO OTHER ANIMAL DOES THIS – NO DOG EXCHANGES BONES WITH ANOTHER.

Adam Smith

The great pleasure of a dog is that you may make a fool of yourself with him and not only will he not scold you, but he will make a fool of himself too.

Samuel Butler

....

NO HUMAN BEING, HOWEVER GREAT, OR POWERFUL, WAS EVER SO FREE AS A FISH.

John Ruskin

....

Deer hunting would be fine sport, if only the deer had guns.

William S. Gilbert

....

What greater gift

THAN THE LOVE

OF A CAT.

Charles Dickens

....

IF A DONKEY BRAY AT YOU,
DON'T BRAY AT HIM.

George Herbert

· ·

A kitten is in the animal world
what a rosebud is in the garden.

Robert Southey

· ·

WHEN THE EAGLES ARE
SILENT, THE PARROTS
BEGIN TO JABBER.

Winston Churchill

Cats have nine lives, which makes them ideal for experimentation.

Jimmy Carr

....

IF YOU ELIMINATE SMOKING
AND GAMBLING, YOU
WILL BE AMAZED TO FIND
THAT ALMOST ALL AN
ENGLISHMAN'S PLEASURES
CAN BE, AND MOSTLY ARE,
SHARED BY HIS DOG.

George Bernard Shaw

Culture
VULTURES

IT IS NOT HARD TO
UNDERSTAND MODERN ART.
IF IT HANGS ON A WALL
IT'S A PAINTING, AND IF
YOU CAN WALK AROUND
IT IT'S A SCULPTURE.

Tom Stoppard

....

The length of a film should be
directly related to the endurance
of the human bladder.

Alfred Hitchcock

....

ART, LIKE MORALITY,
CONSISTS OF DRAWING
THE LINE SOMEWHERE.

G. K. Chesterton

··

Rules and models
DESTROY
GENIUS AND ART.

William Hazlitt

··

Acting is merely the art of keeping a large group of people from coughing.

Ralph Richardson

....

FINE ART IS THAT IN WHICH THE HAND, THE HEAD AND THE HEART OF MAN GO TOGETHER.

John Ruskin

....

Acting is not very hard. The most important things are to be able to laugh and cry.

Glenda Jackson

ANYTHING SIMPLE
ALWAYS INTERESTS ME.

David Hockney

....

Writing about music is like dancing
about architecture – it's a really
stupid thing to want to do.

Elvis Costello

....

I KNOW NOT, SIR, WHETHER
BACON WROTE THE WORKS
OF SHAKESPEARE, BUT IF
HE DID NOT IT SEEMS TO
ME THAT HE MISSED THE
OPPORTUNITY OF HIS LIFE.

J. M. Barrie

History has remembered the kings and warriors, because they destroyed; art has remembered the people, because they created.

William Morris

....

LYING IN BED WOULD BE AN ALTOGETHER PERFECT AND SUPREME EXPERIENCE IF ONLY ONE HAD A COLOURED PENCIL LONG ENOUGH TO DRAW ON THE CEILING.

G. K. Chesterton

....

You just pick up a chord, go twang, and you've got music.

Sid Vicious

WITHOUT TRADITION, ART IS
A FLOCK OF SHEEP WITHOUT
A SHEPHERD. WITHOUT
INNOVATION, IT IS A CORPSE.

Winston Churchill

....

A jazz musician is a juggler who
uses harmonies instead of oranges.

Benny Green

....

WHEN LOVE AND SKILL
WORK TOGETHER, EXPECT
A MASTERPIECE.

John Ruskin

The moral of film-making
in Britain is that you will
be screwed by
the weather.

Hugh Grant

It is a mistake for a sculptor or a painter to speak or write very often about his job. It releases tension needed for his work.

Henry Moore

....

I UNDERSTAND THE INVENTOR OF THE BAGPIPES WAS INSPIRED WHEN HE SAW A MAN CARRYING AN INDIGNANT, ASTHMATIC PIG UNDER HIS ARM. UNFORTUNATELY, THE MAN-MADE SOUND NEVER EQUALLED THE PURITY OF THE SOUND ACHIEVED BY THE PIG.

Alfred Hitchcock

Music is the wine that fills
the cup of silence.

Robert Fripp

....

THERE IS A CERTAIN DARKNESS,
A LYRICAL DARKNESS, IN
THE WELSH CHARACTER
AND THAT IS VERY GOOD
FOR CREATING ART.

Rob Brydon

....

Comedy is simply a funny
way of being serious.

Peter Ustinov

Eye
OF THE
BEHOLDER

THE PROBLEM WITH BEAUTY
IS THAT IT'S LIKE BEING BORN
RICH AND GETTING POORER.

Joan Collins

....

My face looks like a wedding
cake left out in the rain.

W. H. Auden

....

BEAUTY IS ALL VERY
WELL AT FIRST SIGHT; BUT
WHOEVER LOOKS AT IT
WHEN IT HAS BEEN IN THE
HOUSE THREE DAYS?

George Bernard Shaw

A witty woman is a treasure;
a witty beauty is a power.

George Meredith

....

THE HUMAN SOUL
NEEDS ACTUAL BEAUTY
MORE THAN BREAD.

D. H. Lawrence

....

Beauty is an ecstasy; it is as
simple as hunger… It is like
the perfume of a rose: you
can smell it and that is all.

W. Somerset Maugham

How goodness
HEIGHTENS
BEAUTY!

Hannah More

THERE'S MORE TO LIFE THAN CHEEKBONES.

Kate Winslet

....

Beauty is an outward gift which is seldom despised, except by those to whom it has been refused.

Edward Gibbon

....

YOU CAN TAKE NO CREDIT FOR BEAUTY AT 16. BUT IF YOU ARE BEAUTIFUL AT 60, IT WILL BE YOUR SOUL'S OWN DOING.

Marie Stopes

The best part of beauty is that which no picture can express.

Francis Bacon

．．．．．．．．．．．．．．．．．．．．．．．．．．．．．．

IT IS HARD, IF NOT IMPOSSIBLE, TO SNUB A BEAUTIFUL WOMAN – THEY REMAIN BEAUTIFUL AND THE SNUB RECOILS.

Winston Churchill

．．．．．．．．．．．．．．．．．．．．．．．．．．．．．．

The absence of flaw in beauty is itself a flaw.

Henry Havelock Ellis

A POOR BEAUTY FINDS MORE
LOVERS THAN HUSBANDS.

George Herbert

....

Gussie, a glutton for punishment,
stared at himself in the mirror.

P. G. Wodehouse

....

LOVE BUILT ON BEAUTY,
SOON AS BEAUTY, DIES.

John Donne

To look almost pretty is an acquisition of higher delight to a girl who has been looking plain for the first 15 years of her life than a beauty from her cradle can ever receive.

Jane Austen

....

BEAUTY IS NATURE'S COIN, MUST NOT BE HOARDED, BUT MUST BE CURRENT, AND THE GOOD THEREOF CONSISTS IN MUTUAL AND PARTAKEN BLISS.

John Milton

It is well known that Beauty does not look with a good grace on the timid advances of Humour.

W. Somerset Maugham

....

BEAUTY IS THE FIRST PRESENT NATURE GIVES TO WOMEN AND THE FIRST IT TAKES AWAY.

Fay Weldon

....

It has been said that a pretty face is a passport. But it's not, it's a visa, and it runs out fast.

Julie Burchill

Plainness has its peculiar temptations quite as much as beauty.

George Eliot

NONSENSE AND BEAUTY
HAVE CLOSE CONNECTIONS.

E. M. Forster

....

Familiarity is a magician that is cruel
to beauty but kind to ugliness.

Ouida

....

IT IS ONLY SHALLOW
PEOPLE WHO DO NOT
JUDGE BY APPEARANCES.

Oscar Wilde

Under

THE

COVERS

The Englishman can get along with sex quite perfectly so long as he can pretend that it isn't sex but something else.

James Agate

....

FOR FLAVOUR, INSTANT SEX WILL NEVER SUPERSEDE THE STUFF YOU HAVE TO PEEL AND COOK.

Quentin Crisp

....

There is hardly anyone whose sexual life, if it were broadcast, would not fill the world at large with surprise and horror.

W. Somerset Maugham

YOU HAVE TO SEE THE SEX
ACT COMICALLY, AS A CHILD.

W. H. Auden

....

I've only slept with men I've
been married to. How many
women can make that claim?

Elizabeth Taylor

....

IF SOMEONE HAD TOLD ME
YEARS AGO THAT SHARING
A SENSE OF HUMOUR WAS
SO VITAL TO PARTNERSHIPS,
I COULD HAVE AVOIDED
A LOT OF SEX.

Kate Beckinsale

ZZZ

ZZZ

ZZZ

ZZZ

Laugh and the world
laughs with you. Snore
and you sleep alone.

Anthony Burgess

Quite frankly, if you bed
people of below-stairs class,
they go to the papers.

Jane Clark

....

MAKE LOVE TO EVERY WOMAN
YOU MEET; IF YOU GET FIVE
PER CENT OF YOUR OUTLAY
IT'S A GOOD INVESTMENT.

Arnold Bennett

....

I can still enjoy sex at 74 – I
live at 75 so it's no distance.

Bob Monkhouse

WOMEN NEED TO FEEL LOVED
TO HAVE SEX. MEN NEED TO
HAVE SEX TO FEEL LOVED. HOW
DO WE EVER GET STARTED?

Billy Connolly

....

Older women are best, because
they always think they may be
doing it for the last time.

Ian Fleming

....

I'M A SEX MACHINE TO
BOTH GENDERS. IT'S ALL
VERY EXHAUSTING. I
NEED A LOT OF SLEEP.

Rupert Everett

Continental people have sex lives;
the English have hot-water bottles.

Georges Mikes

....

FOR A LONG TIME, I
THOUGHT *COQ AU VIN*
MEAN LOVE IN A LORRY.

Victoria Wood

....

I know it does make people
happy, but to me it is just
like having a cup of tea.

Cynthia Paine

ALL THIS FUSS ABOUT SLEEPING
TOGETHER. FOR PHYSICAL
PLEASURE I'D SOONER GO
TO MY DENTIST ANY DAY.

Evelyn Waugh

....

You know, of course, that the
Tasmanians, who never committed
adultery, are now extinct.

W. Somerset Maugham

....

LITERATURE IS MOSTLY ABOUT
HAVING SEX AND NOT MUCH
ABOUT HAVING CHILDREN; LIFE
IS THE OTHER WAY AROUND.

David Lodge

Sex is a SHORTCUT TO EVERYTHING.

Anne Cumming

Prattle
OF THE
SEXES

Men can never experience the pain of childbirth. They can if you hit them in the goolies for 14 hours.

Jo Brand

....

WIVES ARE YOUNG MEN'S MISTRESSES; COMPANIONS FOR MIDDLE AGE; AND OLD MEN'S NURSES.

Francis Bacon

....

Between men and women there is no friendship possible. There is passion, enmity, worship, love, but no friendship.

Oscar Wilde

SURE MEN WERE BORN TO LIE, AND WOMEN TO BELIEVE THEM!

John Gay

....

Men act and women appear. Men look at women. Women watch themselves being looked at.

John Berger

....

SOME OF MY BEST LEADING MEN HAVE BEEN DOGS AND HORSES.

Elizabeth Taylor

A woman, especially if she has the misfortune of knowing anything, should conceal it as well as she can.

Jane Austen

....

THE MAN'S DESIRE IS FOR THE WOMAN; BUT THE WOMAN'S DESIRE IS RARELY OTHER THAN FOR THE DESIRE OF THE MAN.

Samuel Taylor Coleridge

....

Men are judged as the sum of their parts while women are judged as some of their parts.

Julie Burchill

I EXPECT THAT WOMAN
WILL BE THE LAST THING
CIVILISED BY MAN.

George Meredith

....

There are always women who
will take men on their own
terms. If I were a man I wouldn't
bother to change while there
are women like that around.

Ann Oakley

....

AS USUAL, THERE IS A GREAT
WOMAN BEHIND EVERY IDIOT.

John Lennon

The cocks may crow, but it's
the hen that lays the egg.

Margaret Thatcher

....

MEN ARE GENTLE, HONEST
AND STRAIGHTFORWARD.
WOMEN ARE CONVOLUTED,
DECEPTIVE AND DANGEROUS.

Erin Pizzey

....

It is difficult for a woman
to define her feelings in a
language which is chiefly made
by men to express theirs.

Thomas Hardy

CLEVER AND ATTRACTIVE
WOMEN DO NOT WANT TO
VOTE; THEY ARE WILLING TO
LET MEN GOVERN AS LONG
AS THEY GOVERN MEN.

George Bernard Shaw

....

A man may keep a woman,
but not his estate.

Samuel Richardson

....

MOST OF US WOMEN LIKE
MEN, YOU KNOW; IT'S JUST
THAT WE FIND THEM A
CONSTANT DISAPPOINTMENT.

Clare Short

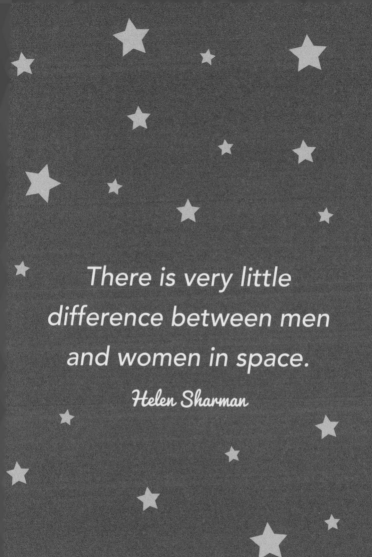

There is very little difference between men and women in space.

Helen Sharman

The war between the sexes is the only one in which both sides regularly sleep with the enemy.

Quentin Crisp

....

THE MAIN DIFFERENCE BETWEEN MEN AND WOMEN IS THAT MEN ARE LUNATICS AND WOMEN ARE IDIOTS.

Rebecca West

....

I would rather trust a woman's instinct than a man's reason.

Stanley Baldwin

THE SILLIEST WOMAN CAN
MANAGE A CLEVER MAN; BUT
IT NEEDS A CLEVER WOMAN
TO MANAGE A FOOL.

Rudyard Kipling

. . . .

If women were as fastidious as
men, morally or physically, there
would be an end of the race.

George Bernard Shaw

. . . .

ONE HALF OF THE WORLD
CANNOT UNDERSTAND THE
PLEASURES OF THE OTHER.

Jane Austen

I don't suppose any man has ever understood any woman since the beginning of things.

H. G. Wells

....

WOMEN HAVE A MUCH BETTER TIME THAN MEN IN THIS WORLD; THERE ARE FAR MORE THINGS FORBIDDEN TO THEM.

Oscar Wilde

Below
THE
BELT

This woman did not fly to extremes; she lived there.

Quentin Crisp

....

SHE HAD MUCH IN COMMON WITH HITLER, ONLY NO MOUSTACHE.

Noël Coward

....

He brings to the fierce struggle of politics the tepid enthusiasm of a lazy summer afternoon at a cricket match.

Aneurin Bevan on Clement Attlee

THE RIGHT HONOURABLE GENTLEMAN IS REMINISCENT OF A POKER. THE ONLY DIFFERENCE IS THAT A POKER GIVES OFF THE OCCASIONAL SIGNS OF WARMTH.

Benjamin Disraeli on Robert Peel

....

There are two ways to dislike poetry: one is to dislike it; the other is to read Pope.

Oscar Wilde

....

NATURE, NOT CONTENT WITH DENYING HIM THE ABILITY TO THINK, HAS ENDOWED HIM WITH THE ABILITY TO WRITE.

A. E. Housman

The tautness of his face sours ripe grapes.

William Shakespeare

She was a large woman
who seemed not so much
dressed as upholstered.

J. M. Barrie

....

SHE PLUNGED INTO A SEA OF
PLATITUDES, AND WITH THE
POWERFUL BREASTSTROKE
OF A CHANNEL SWIMMER,
MADE HER CONFIDENT
WAY TOWARDS THE WHITE
CLIFFS OF THE OBVIOUS.

W. Somerset Maugham

....

He had occasional flashes of
silence that made his conversation
perfectly delightful.

Sydney Smith on Lord Macauley

THOU HAST NO MORE BRAIN
THAN I HAVE IN MINE ELBOWS.

William Shakespeare

....

You've got the subtlety
of a bullfrog.

H. G. Wells

....

WHY DON'T YOU GET A
HAIRCUT? YOU LOOK LIKE
A CHRYSANTHEMUM.

P. G. Wodehouse

He couldn't see a belt
without hitting below it.

Margot Asquith on David Lloyd George

....

WHY DON'T YOU WRITE
BOOKS PEOPLE CAN READ?

Nora Joyce to her husband James Joyce

....

Only dull people are
brilliant at breakfast.

Oscar Wilde

IS HE JUST DOING A BAD
ELVIS POUT, OR WAS HE
BORN THAT WAY?

Freddie Mercury on Billy Idol

....

He would kill his own mother just so
that he could use her skin to make
a drum to beat his own praises.

Margot Asquith on Winston Churchill

....

DID YOUR MOTHER NEVER
TELL YOU NOT TO DRINK
ON AN EMPTY HEAD?

Billy Connolly

His impact on history would be
no more than the whiff of scent
on a lady's handkerchief.

David Lloyd George on Arthur Balfour

....

DO THOU AMEND THY FACE,
AND I'LL AMEND MY LIFE.

William Shakespeare

....

If Kitchener was not a great man,
he was at least, a great poster.

Margot Asquith

· ·

A gentleman is

NEVER RUDE EXCEPT

ON PURPOSE.

Christopher Hitchens

· ·

I SEE HER AS ONE GREAT
STAMPEDE OF LIPS DIRECTED
AT THE NEAREST DERRIÈRE.

Noël Coward

....

In defeat unbeatable; in
victory unbearable.

Winston Churchill on Bernard Montgomery

....

IF I SAY THAT HE IS EXTREMELY
STUPID, I DON'T MEAN THAT
IN A DEROGATORY SENSE.
I SIMPLY MEAN THAT HE'S
NOT VERY INTELLIGENT.

Alan Bennett

Cutting

A

DASH

One should either be a work
of art, or wear a work of art.

Oscar Wilde

....

IF YOU CAN'T BE BETTER
THAN YOUR COMPETITION,
JUST DRESS BETTER.

Anna Wintour

....

What a deformed thief
this fashion is.

William Shakespeare

WHEN A POPULAR
PHENOMENON REACHES
THE COVER OF *TIME*, IT IS
ALREADY OUT OF FASHION.

Richard Holloway

....

Fashion is what you adopt when
you don't know who you are.

Quentin Crisp

....

A FINE COAT IS BUT A
LIVERY WHEN THE PERSON
WHO WEARS IT DISCOVERS
NO HIGHER SENSE THAN
THAT OF A FOOTMAN.

Joseph Addison

As to matters of dress, I would recommend one never to be first in the fashion nor the last out of it.

John Wesley

· ·

I NEVER CARED FOR FASHION MUCH, AMUSING LITTLE SEAMS AND WITTY LITTLE PLEATS: IT WAS THE GIRLS I LIKED.

David Bailey

· ·

One had as good be out of the world, as out of the fashion.

Colley Cibber

If a woman rebels against high-heeled shoes, she should take care to do it in a very smart hat.

George Bernard Shaw

IT'S NOT A CONCERT YOU ARE
SEEING; IT'S A FASHION SHOW.

Freddie Mercury

....

When someone says that lime-green
is the new black for this season, you
just want to tell them to get a life.

Bruce Oldfield

....

OH, NEVER MIND THE
FASHION. WHEN ONE HAS A
STYLE OF ONE'S OWN, IT IS
ALWAYS 20 TIMES BETTER.

Margaret Oliphant

Looking good and dressing
well is a necessity. Having
a purpose in life is not.

Oscar Wilde

....

IT IS NOT EVERY MAN
WHO CAN AFFORD TO
WEAR A SHABBY COAT.

Charles Caleb Colton

....

I'm not here to make people
look like a sack of potatoes.

Alexander McQueen

A well-tied tie is the **FIRST SERIOUS** STEP IN LIFE.

Oscar Wilde

To Have
AND
TO HOLD

Marriage is a very good thing,
but I think it's a mistake to
make a habit out of it.

W. Somerset Maugham

....

ONE SHOULD ALWAYS BE IN
LOVE. THAT IS THE REASON
ONE SHOULD NEVER MARRY.

Oscar Wilde

....

It is a woman's business to get
married… and a man's to keep
unmarried as long as possible.

George Bernard Shaw

ONE WAS NEVER MARRIED, AND
THAT'S HIS HELL; ANOTHER
IS, AND THAT'S HIS PLAGUE.

Robert Burton

....

We were happily married for eight
months. Unfortunately, we were
married for four and a half years.

Nick Faldo

....

IDEALLY, COUPLES NEED
THREE LIVES; ONE FOR HIM,
ONE FOR HER AND ONE
FOR THEM TOGETHER.

Jacqueline Bisset

An archaeologist is the best
husband any woman can have;
the older she gets, the more
interested he is in her.

Agatha Christie

·····································

IRELAND IS A GREAT COUNTRY
TO DIE OR BE MARRIED IN.

Elizabeth Bowen

·····································

The most happy marriage
I can imagine to myself
would be the union of a deaf
man to a blind woman.

Samuel Taylor Coleridge

· ·

Good marriages

ARE MADE IN HEAVEN.

OR SOME SUCH PLACE.

Robert Bolt

· ·

THE CRITICAL PERIOD
IN MATRIMONY IS
BREAKFAST-TIME.

A. P. Herbert

....

Marriage is popular because
it combines the maximum
of temptation with the
maximum of opportunity.

George Bernard Shaw

....

FOR MARRIAGE TO BE A
SUCCESS, EVERY WOMAN
AND EVERY MAN SHOULD
HAVE HER AND HIS OWN
BATHROOM. THE END.

Catherine Zeta-Jones

Marriage may often be a stormy lake, but celibacy is almost always a muddy horse pond.

Thomas Love Peacock

....

MARRIAGE RESEMBLES A PAIR OF SHEARS, SO JOINED THAT THEY CANNOT BE SEPARATED; OFTEN MOVING IN OPPOSITE DIRECTIONS, YET ALWAYS PUNISHING ANYONE WHO COMES BETWEEN THEM.

Sidney Smith

....

Bachelors have consciences, married men have wives.

Samuel Johnson

MARRIAGE IS A WONDERFUL INVENTION; BUT THEN AGAIN, SO IS THE PUNCTURE REPAIR KIT.

Billy Connolly

....

Of course, I do have a slight advantage over the rest of you. It helps in a pinch to be able to remind your bride that you gave up a throne for her.

Edward, Duke of Windsor (formerly King Edward VIII)

....

HAPPINESS IN MARRIAGE IS ENTIRELY A MATTER OF CHANCE.

Jane Austen

With
FRIENDS
LIKE THAT

Thy friendship oft has made
my heart to ache; do be my
enemy, for friendship's sake.

William Blake

....

I PREFER ACQUAINTANCES TO
FRIENDS. THEY DON'T EXPECT
YOU TO CALL OR GO TO THEIR
CHILDREN'S WEDDINGS.

A. A. Gill

....

Most people enjoy the inferiority
of their best friends.

Lord Chesterfield

A friend is
A GIFT YOU GIVE
YOURSELF.

Robert Louis Stevenson

PROMISE ME YOU'LL ALWAYS
REMEMBER: YOU'RE BRAVER
THAN YOU BELIEVE, AND
STRONGER THAN YOU
SEEM, AND SMARTER
THAN YOU THINK.

A. A. Milne

. . . .

Friendship is certainly the
finest balm for the pangs
of disappointed love.

Jane Austen

. . . .

WHERE MINDS DIFFER
AND OPINIONS SWERVE
THERE IS SCANT A FRIEND
IN THAT COMPANY.

Queen Elizabeth I

What do we live for, if not to make life less difficult for each other?

George Eliot

· ·

A BROTHER MAY NOT BE A FRIEND, BUT A FRIEND WILL ALWAYS BE A BROTHER.

Samuel Richardson

· ·

An acquaintance that begins with a compliment is sure to develop into a real friendship.

Oscar Wilde

SOME PEOPLE GO TO
PRIESTS; OTHERS TO POETRY;
I TO MY FRIENDS.

Virginia Woolf

....

True friendship is like sound
health; the value of it is seldom
known until it be lost.

Charles Caleb Colton

....

I AM A HOARDER OF TWO
THINGS: DOCUMENTS
AND TRUSTED FRIENDS.

Muriel Spark

He's my friend that speaks
well of me behind my back.

Thomas Fuller

....

FRIENDSHIP IS LIKE MONEY,
EASIER MADE THAN KEPT.

Samuel Butler

....

Which of all my important
nothings shall I tell you first?

Jane Austen

Friendship

is love

without wings.

Lord Byron

TRUE FRIENDS STAB YOU IN THE FRONT.

Oscar Wilde

....

If a man does not make new acquaintance as he advances through life, he will soon find himself left alone. A man, Sir, should keep his friendship in constant repair.

Samuel Johnson

....

YOU FIND OUT WHO YOUR REAL FRIENDS ARE WHEN YOU'RE INVOLVED IN A SCANDAL.

Elizabeth Taylor

It's What
YOU
MAKE IT

Life, you know, is rather like
opening a tin of sardines. We are
all of us looking for the key.

Alan Bennett

....

THE LIFE OF EVERY MAN
IS A DIARY IN WHICH HE
MEANS TO WRITE ONE STORY,
AND WRITES ANOTHER.

J. M. Barrie

....

The world's a stage, but
the play is badly cast.

Oscar Wilde

LIFE IS SO CONSTRUCTED
THAT AN EVENT DOES
NOT, CANNOT, WILL NOT,
MATCH THE EXPECTATION.

Charlotte Brontë

....

The trouble with the world is
that the stupid are cocksure and
the intelligent full of doubt.

Bertrand Russell

....

LIFE WAS A FUNNY THING
THAT HAPPENED TO ME ON
THE WAY TO THE GRAVE.

Quentin Crisp

The trick in life is learning
how to deal with it.

Helen Mirren

....

LIFE IS WASTED
ON THE LIVING.

Douglas Adams

....

We have employment assigned
to us for every circumstance
in life. When we are alone, we
have our thoughts to watch;
in the family, our tempers; and
in company, our tongues.

Hannah More

· ·

life is one long

PROCESS OF

GETTING TIRED.

Samuel Butler

· ·

LIFE IS A LONG LESSON IN HUMILITY.

J. M. Barrie

....

When we are born, we
cry that we are come
To this great stage of fools.

William Shakespeare

....

LIFE IS WHAT HAPPENS TO YOU WHILE YOU'RE BUSY MAKING OTHER PLANS.

John Lennon

Man alone is born crying, lives complaining, and dies disappointed.

Samuel Johnson

....

MY SCHOOL DAYS WERE THE HAPPIEST DAYS OF MY LIFE; WHICH SHOULD GIVE YOU SOME INDICATION OF THE MISERY I'VE ENDURED OVER THE PAST 25 YEARS.

Paul Merton

....

To live is the rarest thing in the world. Most people exist, that is all.

George Orwell

WE MAKE A LIVING BY WHAT
WE GET, BUT WE MAKE A
LIFE BY WHAT WE GIVE.

Winston Churchill

....

Life is a sexually transmitted
disease and the mortality rate
is one hundred per cent.

R. D. Laing

Thicker
THAN
WATER

After a good dinner one
can forgive anybody, even
one's own relations.

Oscar Wilde

....

THE PLACE OF THE FATHER
IN THE MODERN SUBURBAN
FAMILY IS A VERY SMALL
ONE, PARTICULARLY
IF HE PLAYS GOLF.

Bertrand Russell

....

Whether family life is physically
harmful is still in dispute.

Keith Waterhouse

WE CAME INTO THE
WORLD LIKE BROTHER AND
BROTHER; AND NOW LET'S
GO HAND IN HAND, NOT
ONE BEFORE ANOTHER.

William Shakespeare

....

If a man's character is to be abused,
say what you will, there's nobody
like a relation to do the business.

William Makepeace Thackeray

....

IMPORTANT FAMILIES ARE
LIKE POTATOES. THE BEST
PARTS ARE UNDERGROUND.

Francis Bacon

He that has no fools,
knaves, nor beggars in his
family, was begot by a
flash of lightning.

Thomas Fuller

If you cannot get rid of the
family skeleton, you may
as well make it dance.

George Bernard Shaw

∙∙∙∙∙∙∙∙∙∙∙∙∙∙∙∙∙∙∙∙∙∙∙∙∙∙∙∙∙∙∙∙∙∙∙∙∙∙

YOU KNOW WHAT THEY SAY, IF
AT FIRST YOU DON'T SUCCEED,
YOU'RE NOT THE ELDEST SON.

Stephen Fry

∙∙∙∙∙∙∙∙∙∙∙∙∙∙∙∙∙∙∙∙∙∙∙∙∙∙∙∙∙∙∙∙∙∙∙∙∙∙

The awe and dread with which the
untutored savage contemplates
his mother-in-law are amongst the
most familiar facts of anthropology.

James George Frazer

FAMILY JOKES, THOUGH
RIGHTLY CURSED BY
STRANGERS, ARE THE
BOND THAT KEEPS MOST
FAMILIES ALIVE.

Stella Benson

....

The great advantage of living in
a large family is that early lesson
of life's essential unfairness.

Nancy Mitford

By
THE
BOOK

You simply sit down at
the typewriter, open your
veins and bleed.

Red Smith on writing

....

SOME BOOKS ARE TO BE
TASTED, OTHERS TO BE
SWALLOWED, AND SOME FEW
TO BE CHEWED AND DIGESTED.

Francis Bacon

....

I've always believed in writing
without a collaborator, because
where two people are writing
the same book, each believes
he gets all the worries and
only half the royalties.

Agatha Christie

HOW LITTLE OUR LIBRARIES
COST US AS COMPARED WITH
OUR LIQUOR CELLARS.

John Lubbock

....

Literature is the art of writing
something that will be read twice;
journalism will be grasped at once.

Cyril Connolly

....

NO HUMAN BEING EVER
SPOKE OF SCENERY FOR ABOVE
TWO MINUTES AT A TIME,
WHICH MAKES ME SUSPECT
THAT WE HEAR TOO MUCH
OF IT IN LITERATURE.

Robert Louis Stevenson

I hate vulgar realism in literature. The man who could call a spade a spade should be compelled to use one. It is the only thing he is fit for.

Oscar Wilde

....

A HISTORICAL ROMANCE IS THE ONLY KIND OF BOOK WHERE CHASTITY REALLY COUNTS.

Barbara Cartland

....

You don't write because you want to say something, you write because you've got something to say.

F. Scott Fitzgerald

THE BEAUTY OF THE BRAIN
IS THAT YOU CAN STILL
BE AS GREEDY AS YOU
LIKE FOR KNOWLEDGE
AND IT DOESN'T SHOW.

Stephen Fry

....

Better to write for yourself and
have no public, than to write for
the public and have no self.

Cyril Connolly

....

IF YOU CANNOT SAY WHAT
YOU ARE GOING TO SAY IN
20 MINUTES YOU OUGHT
TO GO AWAY AND WRITE
A BOOK ABOUT IT.

Lord Brabazon

We read to know
THAT WE ARE
NOT ALONE.

C. S. Lewis

Everything is useful to a
writer, you see – every scrap,
even the longest and most
boring of luncheon parties.

Graham Greene

....

A GREAT MANY PEOPLE NOW
READING AND WRITING
WOULD BE BETTER EMPLOYED
KEEPING RABBITS.

Edith Sitwell

....

The sheer complexity of writing
a play always had dazzled me.
In an effort to understand
it, I became a critic.

Kenneth Tynan

IT IS ALL VERY WELL TO BE
ABLE TO WRITE BOOKS, BUT
CAN YOU WAGGLE YOUR EARS?

J. M. Barrie

....

There is a great discovery still
to be made in literature, that
of paying literary men by the
quantity they do not write.

Thomas Carlyle

....

WHILE AN AUTHOR IS YET
LIVING WE ESTIMATE HIS
POWERS BY HIS WORST
PERFORMANCE, AND
WHEN HE IS DEAD WE
RATE THEM BY HIS BEST.

Samuel Johnson

A pen is to me as a
beak is to a hen.

J. R. R. Tolkien

....

ONE HATES AN AUTHOR
THAT'S ALL AUTHOR.

Lord Byron

....

Let every bookworm, when in
any fragrant, scarce, old tome
he discovers a sentence, a
story, an illustration, that does
his heart good, hasten to give
it the widest circulation that
newspapers and magazines, penny
and half-penny, can afford.

Samuel Taylor Coleridge

I CAN'T WRITE A BOOK
COMMENSURATE WITH
SHAKESPEARE, BUT I CAN
WRITE A BOOK BY ME.

Walter Raleigh

. . . .

Unprovided with original learning,
unformed in the habits of thinking,
unskilled in the arts of composition,
I resolved to write a book.

Edward Gibbon

. . . .

POETRY: THE BEST WORDS
IN THE BEST ORDER.

Samuel Taylor Coleridge

Johnny
FOREIGNER

Admiration for ourselves and our institutions is too often measured by our contempt and dislike for foreigners.

William Ralph Inge

....

AMERICA IS A LARGE FRIENDLY DOG IN A SMALL ROOM. EVERY TIME IT WAGS ITS TAIL, IT KNOCKS OVER A CHAIR.

Arnold Joseph Toynbee

....

I can't even spell spaghetti, never mind talk Italian. How could I tell an Italian to get the ball? He might grab mine.

Brian Clough

THE IRISH ARE A FAIR
PEOPLE; THEY NEVER SPEAK
WELL OF ONE ANOTHER.

Samuel Johnson

....

A man travels the world in
search of what he needs and
returns home to find it.

George Moore

....

TRAVEL, IN THE YOUNGER
SORT, IS A PART OF
EDUCATION; IN THE ELDER,
A PART OF EXPERIENCE.

Francis Bacon

An English man DOES NOT TRAVEL TO SEE ENGLISH MEN.

Laurence Sterne

England is a paradise for women and hell for horses; Italy is a paradise for horses, hell for women, as the diverb goes.

Robert Burton

....

A CUT-GLASS ENGLISH ACCENT CAN FOOL UNSUSPECTING AMERICANS INTO DETECTING A BRILLIANCE THAT ISN'T THERE.

Stephen Fry

....

In Mexico, an air conditioner is called a politician because it makes a lot of noise but doesn't work very well.

Len Deighton

THEY SAY TRAVEL BROADENS
THE MIND; BUT YOU
MUST HAVE THE MIND.

G. K. Chesterton

....

They pour themselves one
over the other like so much
melted butter over parsnips.

D. H. Lawrence on Italians

....

I LOVE AMERICANS, BUT NOT
WHEN THEY TRY TO TALK
FRENCH. WHAT A BLESSING
IT IS THAT THEY NEVER
TRY TO TALK ENGLISH.

Saki

San Francisco is a mad city –
inhabited for the most part by
perfectly insane people whose
women are of remarkable beauty.

Rudyard Kipling

....

I DON'T LIKE SWITZERLAND: IT
HAS PRODUCED NOTHING BUT
THEOLOGIANS AND WAITERS.

Oscar Wilde

....

Apart from cheese and
tulips, the main product of
the country is advocaat, a
drink made from lawyers.

Alan Coren on the Netherlands

People travel for
the same reason they
collect works of art:
because the best
people do it.

Aldous Huxley

When
THEIR LIPS
MOVE

A LOT HAS BEEN SAID ABOUT
POLITICIANS; SOME OF IT
COMPLIMENTARY, BUT
MOST OF IT ACCURATE.

Eric Idle

....

The wisdom of hindsight, so
useful to historians and indeed
to authors of memoirs, is sadly
denied to practising politicians.

Margaret Thatcher

....

POLITICS ARE VERY MUCH LIKE
WAR. WE MAY EVEN HAVE TO
USE POISON GAS AT TIMES.

Winston Churchill

A parliament is nothing less than a big meeting of more or less idle people.

Walter Bagehot

....

THE LONGEST SUICIDE NOTE IN HISTORY.

Labour MP Gerald Kaufman on his party's 1983 election manifesto

....

The ego has landed.

Frank Dobson on Ken Livingstone

IF THE WORD 'NO' WAS
REMOVED FROM THE ENGLISH
LANGUAGE, IAN PAISLEY
WOULD BE SPEECHLESS.

John Hume

....

If there is one truth of politics, it
is that there are always a dozen
good reasons for doing nothing.

John le Carré

....

HE KNOWS NOTHING; AND
HE THINKS HE KNOWS
EVERYTHING. THAT
POINTS CLEARLY TO A
POLITICAL CAREER.

George Bernard Shaw

Healey's first law of politics: when you're in a hole, stop digging.

Denis Healey

I am humble enough to recognise
that I have made mistakes, but
politically astute enough to
have forgotten what they are.

Michael Heseltine

· ·

DEMOCRACY MEANS
SIMPLY THE BLUDGEONING
OF THE PEOPLE BY THE
PEOPLE FOR THE PEOPLE.

Oscar Wilde

· ·

When I want a peerage, I shall
buy it like an honest man.

Lord Northcliffe

WHEN GREAT MEN GET
DRUNK WITH A THEORY,
IT IS THE LITTLE MEN WHO
HAVE THE HEADACHE.

Lord Salisbury

....

The best time to listen to a
politician is when he's on a
stump on a street corner in
the rain late at night when he's
exhausted. Then he doesn't lie.

Theodore H. White

....

I REMAIN JUST ONE THING,
AND ONE THING ONLY, AND
THAT IS A CLOWN. IT PLACES
ME ON A FAR HIGHER PLANE
THAN ANY POLITICIAN.

Charlie Chaplin

There's nothing so improves the mood of the Party as the imminent execution of a senior colleague.

Alan Clark

. . . .

THE DIFFERENCE BETWEEN A MISFORTUNE AND A CALAMITY IS THIS: IF GLADSTONE FELL INTO THE THAMES, IT WOULD BE A MISFORTUNE. BUT IF SOMEONE DRAGGED HIM OUT AGAIN, THAT WOULD BE A CALAMITY.

Benjamin Disraeli

. . . .

You slam a politician, you make out he's the devil… But his wife loves him, and so did all his mistresses.

Pamela Hansford Johnson

························

Politics
IS A BLOOD
SPORT.

Aneurin Bevan

························

POLITICS IS THE ART OF
LOOKING FOR TROUBLE,
FINDING IT WHETHER IT EXISTS
OR NOT, DIAGNOSING IT
INCORRECTLY, AND APPLYING
THE WRONG REMEDY.

Ernest Benn

....

The politician who never made a
mistake never made a decision.

John Major

....

WE ALL KNOW THAT PRIME
MINISTERS ARE WEDDED TO
THE TRUTH, BUT LIKE OTHER
WEDDED COUPLES THEY
SOMETIMES LIVE APART.

Saki

A politician is a person with whose politics you don't agree; if you agree with him he's a statesman.

David Lloyd George

....

ANYBODY WHO ENJOYS BEING IN THE HOUSE OF COMMONS PROBABLY NEEDS PSYCHIATRIC CARE.

Ken Livingstone

....

You can't be in politics unless you can walk in a room and know in a minute who's for you and who's against you.

Samuel Johnson

Head

OVER

HEELS

Love's like the measles – all the
worse when it comes late in life.

Douglas Jerrold

....

TO FEAR LOVE IS TO FEAR
LIFE, AND THOSE WHO
FEAR LIFE ARE ALREADY
THREE PARTS DEAD.

Bertrand Russell

....

When my love swears that
she is made of truth,
I do believe her though
I know she lies.

William Shakespeare

TO FALL IN LOVE YOU HAVE TO
BE IN THE STATE OF MIND FOR
IT TO TAKE, LIKE A DISEASE.

Nancy Mitford

....

How absurd and delicious to be in
love with somebody younger than
yourself. Everybody should try it.

Barbara Pym

....

LOVE IS ONLY A DIRTY
TRICK PLAYED ON US TO
ACHIEVE CONTINUATION
OF THE SPECIES.

W. Somerset Maugham

A mistress never is nor can
be a friend. While you agree,
you are lovers; and when it is
over, anything but friends.

Lord Byron

. . . .

IF YOU LIVE TO BE A HUNDRED,
I WANT TO LIVE TO BE A
HUNDRED MINUS ONE DAY.

A. A. Milne

. . . .

Love is an act of endless
forgiveness; a tender look
which becomes a habit.

Peter Ustinov

NO WOMAN EVER HATES A
MAN FOR BEING IN LOVE
WITH HER, BUT MANY A
WOMAN HATES A MAN FOR
BEING A FRIEND TO HER.

Alexander Pope

....

Love is a wonderful,
terrible thing.

William Shakespeare

....

LOVE COMES UNSEEN;
WE ONLY SEE IT GO.

Austin Dobson

Whatever our souls are made of, his and mine are the same.

Emily Brontë

Who ever loved that loved
not at first sight?

Christopher Marlowe

....

A LOVING HEART IS
THE BEGINNING OF
ALL KNOWLEDGE.

Thomas Carlyle

....

The simple lack of her is more
to me than others' presence.

Edward Thomas

MEN ALWAYS WANT TO BE
A WOMAN'S FIRST LOVE
– WOMEN LIKE TO BE A
MAN'S LAST ROMANCE.

Oscar Wilde

．．．．．．．．．．．．．．．．．．．．．．．．．．．．．．

**Love is my religion –
I could die for it.**

John Keats

Mind
YOUR
Ps AND Qs

In England, we have such good manners that if someone says something impolite, the police will get involved.

Russell Brand

....

MANNERS ARE ESPECIALLY THE NEED OF THE PLAIN. THE PRETTY CAN GET AWAY WITH ANYTHING.

Evelyn Waugh

....

The English are polite by telling lies. The Americans are polite by telling the truth.

Malcolm Bradbury

A MAN'S OWN GOOD BREEDING IS HIS BEST SECURITY AGAINST OTHER PEOPLE'S ILL MANNERS.

Lord Chesterfield

....

Talk to every woman as if you loved her, and to every man as if he bored you, and at the end of your first season you will have the reputation of possessing the most perfect social tact.

Oscar Wilde

....

IT IS MORE COMFORTABLE FOR ME, IN THE LONG RUN, TO BE RUDE THAN POLITE.

Wyndham Lewis

In proceeding to the dining
room, the gentleman gives one
arm to the lady he escorts – it
is unusual to offer both.

Lewis Carroll

....

I DO NOT WANT PEOPLE TO
BE VERY AGREEABLE, AS IT
SAVES ME THE TROUBLE OF
LIKING THEM A GREAT DEAL.

Jane Austen

....

And though it is much to
be a nobleman, it is more
to be a gentleman.

Anthony Trollope

....

Civility costs

NOTHING AND BUYS

EVERYTHING.

Lady Mary Wortley Montagu

....

WHOEVER ONE IS, AND
WHEREVER ONE IS, ONE IS
ALWAYS IN THE WRONG
IF ONE IS RUDE.

Maurice Baring

....

At a dinner party one should
eat wisely but not too well, and
talk well but not too wisely.

W. Somerset Maugham

....

WE DON'T BOTHER MUCH
ABOUT DRESS AND MANNERS
IN ENGLAND, BECAUSE AS A
NATION WE DON'T DRESS WELL
AND WE'VE GOT NO MANNERS.

George Bernard Shaw

The Curse
OF THE
DRINKING
CLASSES

I like work; it fascinates me. I can sit and look at it for hours.

Jerome K. Jerome

....

THE BEST WAY TO APPRECIATE YOUR JOB IS TO IMAGINE YOURSELF WITHOUT ONE.

Oscar Wilde

....

Work with some men is as besetting a sin as idleness.

Samuel Butler

NOTHING IS REALLY WORK
UNLESS YOU WOULD RATHER
BE DOING SOMETHING ELSE.

J. M. Barrie

....

Make lots of money. Enjoy the
work. Operate within the law.
Choose any two of three.

Jack Dee

....

A FOOLPROOF PLAN FOR
NOT GETTING A JOB – SHOW
UP FOR YOUR INTERVIEW
WEARING FLIP-FLOPS.

Alan Davies

I love deadlines. I love
the whooshing noise
they make as they go by.

Douglas Adams

The reward of labour is life.
Is that not enough?

William Morris

....

IF YOU HAVE GREAT TALENTS,
INDUSTRY WILL IMPROVE
THEM: IF YOU HAVE BUT
MODERATE ABILITIES,
INDUSTRY WILL SUPPLY
THEIR DEFICIENCY.

Joshua Reynolds

....

If you want creative workers,
give them enough time to play.

John Cleese

BUSINESS OPPORTUNITIES ARE
LIKE BUSES: THERE'S ALWAYS
ANOTHER ONE COMING.

Richard Branson

. . . .

It is very vulgar to talk about
one's business. Only people
like stockbrokers do that, and
then merely at dinner parties.

Oscar Wilde

. . . .

ONE OF THE SYMPTOMS OF
AN APPROACHING NERVOUS
BREAKDOWN IS THE BELIEF
THAT ONE'S WORK IS
TERRIBLY IMPORTANT.

Bertrand Russell

Set me anything to do as a task,
and it is inconceivable the desire
I have to do something else.

George Bernard Shaw

. . . .

IT IS THE JOB THAT IS NEVER
STARTED THAT TAKES
LONGEST TO FINISH.

J. R. R. Tolkien

Well,
IF YOU
ASK ME...

ADVICE IS SELDOM WELCOME,
AND THOSE WHO NEED IT THE
MOST, LIKE IT THE LEAST.

Lord Chesterfield

....

Remember, you can always
stoop and pick up nothing.

Charlie Chaplin

....

NEVER KEEP UP WITH THE
JONESES. DRAG THEM DOWN
TO YOUR LEVEL. IT'S CHEAPER.

Quentin Crisp

Have the courage to be ignorant of a great number of things, in order to avoid the calamity of being ignorant of everything.

Sydney Smith

....

A LITTLE INACCURACY SOMETIMES SAVES TONS OF EXPLANATION.

Saki

....

Good but rarely came from good advice.

Lord Byron

A sure cure for seasickness is to sit under a tree.

Spike Milligan

THE ONLY WAY TO BE SURE
OF CATCHING A TRAIN IS TO
MISS THE ONE BEFORE IT.

G. K. Chesterton

....

A woman seldom asks advice
before she has bought
her wedding clothes.

Joseph Addison

....

WHEN A MAN WANTS YOUR
ADVICE, HE GENERALLY
WANTS YOUR PRAISE.

Lord Chesterfield

Love all, trust a few,
Do wrong to none.

William Shakespeare

....

DON'T GIVE A WOMAN ADVICE;
ONE SHOULD NEVER GIVE
A WOMAN ANYTHING SHE
CAN'T WEAR IN THE EVENING.

Oscar Wilde

....

The worst men often give
the best advice.

Francis Bacon

....

Never
PUT A SOCK
IN A TOASTER.

Eddie Izzard

....

MODERATION IS A FATAL
THING – NOTHING
SUCCEEDS LIKE EXCESS.

Oscar Wilde

....

I owe my success to having
listened respectfully to the very
best advice, and then going away
and doing the exact opposite.

G. K. Chesterton

....

NEVER TRY TO REASON THE
PREJUDICE OUT OF A MAN.
IT WAS NOT REASONED
INTO HIM, AND CANNOT
BE REASONED OUT.

Sydney Smith

Vice
AND
VIRTUE

The problem with people who have no vices is that generally you can be pretty sure they're going to have some pretty annoying virtues.

Elizabeth Taylor

....

THE GREATEST ART OF A POLITICIAN IS TO RENDER VICE SERVICEABLE TO THE CAUSE OF VIRTUE.

Henry Bolingbroke

....

I was horrified to find the other week that my second son is taking drugs. My very best ones too.

Bob Monkhouse

FOR GOD'S SAKE, IF YOU
SIN, TAKE PLEASURE IN IT,
AND DO IT FOR THE PLEASURE.

Gerald Gould

....

How like herrings and onions our
vices are in the morning after
we have committed them.

Samuel Taylor Coleridge

....

GOOD TASTE IS THE WORST
VICE EVER INVENTED.

Edith Sitwell

Flippancy, the most hopeless
form of intellectual vice.

George Gissing

....

IF THERE WERE NO BAD
PEOPLE, THERE WOULD BE
NO GOOD LAWYERS.

Charles Dickens

....

I always admired virtue – but
I could never imitate it.

King Charles II

IF YOU PRETEND TO BE GOOD,
THE WORLD TAKES YOU VERY
SERIOUSLY. IF YOU PRETEND
TO BE BAD, IT DOESN'T.
SUCH IS THE ASTOUNDING
STUPIDITY OF OPTIMISM.

Oscar Wilde

....

All art is a struggle to be, in a
particular sort of way, virtuous.

Iris Murdoch

....

GOOD AND BAD MEN ARE
EACH LESS SO THAN THEY SEEM.

Samuel Taylor Coleridge

Virtue is more to be feared than vice, because its excesses are not subject to the regulation of conscience.

Adam Smith

....

IF YOU RESOLVE TO GIVE UP SMOKING, DRINKING AND LOVING, YOU DON'T ACTUALLY LIVE LONGER – IT JUST SEEMS LONGER.

Clement Freud

....

Oh, blameless people are always the most exasperating!

George Eliot

I HAVE OFTEN WISHED I
HAD TIME TO CULTIVATE
MODESTY. BUT I AM TOO BUSY
THINKING ABOUT MYSELF.

Edith Sitwell

....

As threshing separates the
wheat from the chaff, so does
affliction purify virtue.

Richard Francis Burton

....

ON THE WHOLE, HUMAN
BEINGS WANT TO BE GOOD,
BUT NOT TOO GOOD, AND
NOT QUITE ALL THE TIME.

George Orwell

What after all is a halo? It's only one more thing to keep clean.

Christopher Fry

....

VICES AND VIRTUES ARE OF A STRANGE NATURE, FOR THE MORE WE HAVE, THE FEWER WE THINK WE HAVE.

Alexander Pope

....

Moderation has been called a virtue to limit the ambition of great men, and to console undistinguished people for their want of fortune and their lack of merit.

Benjamin Disraeli

Goodness is
BEAUTY IN ITS
BEST ESTATE.

Christopher Marlowe

IN ENGLAND THE ONLY
HOMAGE WHICH THEY PAY
TO VIRTUE – IS HYPOCRISY.

Lord Byron

....

Blessed is the man who, having
nothing to say, abstains from giving
us wordy evidence of the fact.

George Eliot

....

THE MOST INFLUENTIAL
OF ALL THE VIRTUES ARE
THOSE WHICH ARE THE
MOST IN REQUEST FOR DAILY
USE. THEY WEAR THE BEST,
AND LAST THE LONGEST.

Samuel Smiles

Drunk

AS A

LORD

CHEAP BOOZE IS A
FALSE ECONOMY.

Christopher Hitchens

....

And wine can of their wits
the wise beguile,
Make the sage frolic, and
the serious smile.

Alexander Pope

....

NO ANIMAL EVER INVENTED
ANYTHING SO BAD AS
DRUNKENNESS – OR SO
GOOD AS DRINK.

G. K. Chesterton

A good local pub has much in
common with a church, except
that a pub is warmer, and
there's more conversation.

William Blake

....

WHEN I PLAYED DRUNKS I HAD
TO REMAIN SOBER BECAUSE I
DIDN'T KNOW HOW TO PLAY
THEM WHEN I WAS DRUNK.

Richard Burton

....

Real ale fans are just like
trainspotters, only drunk.

Christopher Howse

I do not live
IN THE WORLD
OF SOBRIETY.

Oliver Reed

ALCOHOL... IT ENABLES
PARLIAMENT TO DO THINGS
AT ELEVEN AT NIGHT THAT
NO SANE PERSON WOULD DO
AT ELEVEN IN THE MORNING.

George Bernard Shaw

....

The first draught serveth for health,
the second for pleasure, the third
for shame, the fourth for madness.

Walter Raleigh

....

FILL IT UP. I TAKE AS LARGE
DRAUGHTS OF LIQUOR AS
I DID OF LOVE. I HATE A
FLINCHER IN EITHER.

John Gay

This is one of the disadvantages of wine; it makes a man mistake words for thoughts.

Samuel Johnson

....

THE BEST RESEARCH FOR PLAYING A DRUNK IS BEING A BRITISH ACTOR FOR 20 YEARS.

Michael Caine

....

It is widely held that too much wine will dull a man's desire. Indeed it will – in a dull man.

John Osborne

I HAVE TAKEN MORE OUT OF
ALCOHOL THAN ALCOHOL
HAS TAKEN OUT OF ME.

Winston Churchill

....

Drink is the feast of reason
and the flow of soul.

Alexander Pope

....

A TAVERN IS A PLACE
WHERE MADNESS IS SOLD
BY THE BOTTLE.

Jonathan Swift

There are some sluggish men
who are improved by drinking;
as there are fruits that are not
good until they are rotten.

Samuel Johnson

....

I CAN RESIST EVERYTHING
EXCEPT TEMPTATION.

Oscar Wilde

The Youth

OF

TODAY

I AM NOT YOUNG ENOUGH
TO KNOW EVERYTHING.

J. M. Barrie

....

Youth is a wonderful thing. What
a crime to waste it on children.

George Bernard Shaw

....

YOUNG BLOOD MUST
HAVE ITS COURSE, LAD,
AND EVERY DOG HIS DAY.

Charles Kingsley

What Youth deemed crystal,
Age finds out was dew.

Robert Browning

....

THE ARROGANCE OF
AGE MUST SUBMIT TO BE
TAUGHT BY YOUTH.

Edmund Burke

....

There is something so amiable
in the prejudices of a young
mind, that one is sorry to see
them give way to the reception
of more general opinions.

Jane Austen

THE EXCESSES OF OUR YOUTH
ARE CHEQUES WRITTEN
AGAINST OUR AGE AND
THEY ARE PAYABLE WITH
INTEREST 30 YEARS LATER.

Charles Caleb Colton

....

It is an illusion that youth is happy,
an illusion of those who have lost it.

W. Somerset Maugham

....

YOUNG PEOPLE HAVE A
MARVELLOUS FACULTY
OF EITHER DYING OR
ADAPTING THEMSELVES
TO CIRCUMSTANCES.

Samuel Butler

I love children, especially when they cry, because then somebody takes them away.

Nancy Mitford

....

WHAT IS YOUTH EXCEPT A MAN OR A WOMAN BEFORE IT IS READY OR FIT TO BE SEEN?

Evelyn Waugh

....

Human nature is so well disposed towards those who are in interesting situations, that a young person, who either marries or dies, is sure of being kindly spoken of.

Jane Austen

Fame is the
thirst of youth.

Lord Byron

THE TROUBLE WITH CHILDREN IS THAT THEY ARE NOT RETURNABLE.

Quentin Crisp

....

To get back my youth I would do anything in the world, except take exercise, get up early, or be respectable.

Oscar Wilde

....

YOUTH SMILES WITHOUT ANY REASON. IT IS ONE OF ITS CHIEFEST CHARMS.

Thomas Gray

The Way
OF ALL
FLESH

THE IDEA IS TO DIE YOUNG AS LATE AS POSSIBLE.

Ashley Montagu

....

Nothing in his life became him like the leaving it.

William Shakespeare

....

THERE'S NOTHING GLORIOUS IN DYING. ANYONE CAN DO IT.

Johnny Rotten

Nothing except possibly love
and death are of importance, and
even the importance of death is
somewhat ephemeral, as no one
has yet faxed back a reliable report.

Gerald Durrell

....

EITHER THAT WALLPAPER
GOES, OR I DO.

Oscar Wilde on his deathbed

....

I blame myself for my
boyfriend's death. I shot him.

Jo Brand

IN LIVERPOOL, THE DIFFERENCE
BETWEEN A FUNERAL AND A
WEDDING IS ONE LESS DRUNK.

Paul O'Grady

....

I'm trying to die correctly, but
it's very difficult, you know.

Lawrence Durrell

....

HE'D MAKE A
LOVELY CORPSE.

Charles Dickens

Life levels all men. Death
reveals the eminent.

George Bernard Shaw

·····································

I WANT TO DIE LIKE MY
FATHER, PEACEFULLY IN
HIS SLEEP, NOT SCREAMING
AND TERRIFIED, LIKE
HIS PASSENGERS.

Bob Monkhouse

·····································

Most people would rather die
than think; in fact, they do so.

Bertrand Russell

······················

I told
YOU I
WAS ILL.

Spike Milligan's epitaph

······················

BRILLIANT

BRITAIN

A CELEBRATION OF ITS
UNIQUE TRADITIONS AND CUSTOMS

JANE PEYTON

BRILLIANT BRITAIN
A Celebration of its Unique Traditions and Customs

Jane Peyton

ISBN: 978 1 84953 309 6
Hardback
£9.99

Brilliant Britain is an entertaining journey through the quirks, oddities and idiosyncrasies that define our nation and preserve us from the mundane and predictable, such as:

- the royal pomp and pageantry of the State Opening of Parliament and the less well-known swan-upping;

- unusual sports and pastimes, from bog snorkelling to worm charming;

- annual countrywide events including the May Day festivities and the beating of the bounds;

- dialects and slang, provincial foods and a recipe for the perfect chip butty.

This book lifts the lid on a rich heritage of eccentricity and diversity, exploring all that makes Britain brilliant.

If you're interested in finding out more about our books, find us on Facebook at *Summersdale Publishers* and follow us on Twitter at *@Summersdale*.

www.summersdale.com